# TUNBRIDGE WELLS

## The Gentle Aspect

Also by Terence Davis

*The Architecture of John Nash* (Studio, 1960).

*John Nash, The Prince Regent's Architecture*
(Country Life, 1966).

*Great Interiors (Neo-Classicism)*
(Weidenfeld and Nicolson, 1967).

*Rococo* (Orbis, 1973).

*The Gothick Taste* (David and Charles, 1974).

*Frontispiece overleaf*:
No. 8 Cumberland Walk.

# Tunbridge Wells

## The Gentle Aspect

TERENCE DAVIS

*Photographs*
*by*

CHARLES SAUMAREZ SMITH

PHILLIMORE

1976

PHILLIMORE & CO., LTD.,
London and Chichester

*Head Office:* Shopwyke Hall,
Chichester, Sussex, England

ISBN 0 85033 250 8

Set in 11/13pt. Baskerville

Printed in Great Britain by
Butler & Tanner Ltd.,
Frome and London

❦❦❦❦❦

*For G. & I.*
*with gratitude*

⚜⚜⚜⚜⚜

❧❧❧❧❧

'This rural spot its ancient grandeur shows,
When Tumbridge Wells amidst a desert rose . . .'

*from lines written on a table in the Baths, 1820*

❧❧❧❧❧

# Contents

ক্ষক্ষক্ষক্ষক্ষক্ষ

# Illustrations

ঞ঻ঞ঻ঞ঻ঞ঻ঞ঻ঞ঻ঞ঻ঞ঻

*(Numbers in brackets in text refer to illustrations)*

# Acknowledgments

ֆֆֆֆֆֆֆֆ

I would like to thank Sir John Betjeman who first encouraged me to make a study of Tunbridge Wells and the following who have provided information on various aspects of the town's history and building: Mr. Claude Delves, Miss Jean Mauldon, Mr. Richard Sandbach and Mr. Alan Savidge.

Mr. Kenneth Miller and Mr. Philip Whitbourn, vigilant residents, have also made several helpful suggestions for this essay.

Members of the Tunbridge Wells branch of the Royal Institute of British Architects, acknowledged in the list of illustrations, have kindly allowed me to reproduce drawings from their European Architectural Heritage Year broadsheet.

TERENCE DAVIS

Wadhurst,
Sussex
1976

# Preface

৯৯৯৯৯৯৯৯

AT THE END of 1975 I found myself in a small grey room in a Tunbridge Wells hospital with a sudden illness. I give this gratuitous piece of information because the event is partly responsible for the form of this book and helps to explain its sub-title.

For months, like anyone writing a short architectural history of a large town, the problem was what to leave out. I went through periods of suppressing my pet aversions in an attempt to give a 'balanced' picture—the good and the bad living happily together. But, of course, they don't; and the view from the windows of the hospital confirmed this once and for all. One view was literally electrifying—great Christmas lights of every colour filled the motor-cycle showroom in a mutilated 19th-century building next door to a petrol station of average ugliness, equally lit with dazzling lights. The view from the other window did not dim the eyes, merely the spirits: a lop-sided water tank on a corroded metal stand silhouetted against a corrugated iron wall. Every town in the world can offer similar or worse prospects; they simply helped me with my problem of selection and, unimportant as these little scenes were in themselves, they strengthened my aversions in which I had been trying to interest my naturally retrograde and reactionary visual nature: the petrol station that blocks the view of the Common from Mount Sion; the 'Rest Shelter' nearby, resembling a Mediterranean clubhouse, set in a position of great importance with the words 'Ladies and Gentlemen' in gigantic letters; the pathetic parade of shop-fronts on the west side of Mount Pleasant; the Civic Centre set at a ludicrous angle and of the wrong scale and style . . .

Later I was moved into another ward and here the view was in the same direction—towards the motor-cycle shop—but it had vanished out of sight to the left and was replaced by a group of stuccoed Regency houses—one bow-fronted pair with twin doors sharing an attractive fanlight. To the right were the white-painted weather-boarded shops of Mount Ephraim with their balconies of wrought iron. Visually the scene was of an essential, earlier Tunbridge Wells. Only the continual thunder of small and large container vehicles on their way to the coast wrecked this sympathetic and pleasing prospect.

So the gentle, quieter architectural aspects of this remarkable town became more difficult to reject than the 1930s cinema, the new multi-storey car park or the latest office block. Useful as they are, the average visitor to a resort does not seek out the new gasworks; likewise the visitor to Tunbridge Wells. All the buildings illustrated or described exist at the time of writing.

From 1776 when Burr, Sprange, Amsinck, Colbran and others wrote their accounts of Tunbridge Wells, the bare bones of the town could be described adequately in a few short pages. A small, exclusive spa has become a complex residential town. Set on the Kent-Sussex borders in natural scenery of exceptional beauty, a handful of humble cottages and farms has been replaced over the years by buildings of some considerable architectural merit. The great Victorian and Edwardian mansions arranged in private parks testified to the fact that income per head in those days was said to be greater than in any other country town. These buildings succeeded the more modest ones of Decimus Burton and William Willicombe to whom we owe large areas of landscaping and street planning and represent some of the last monuments to Victorian wealth. The history of the town has been written many times[1] but an attempt to isolate some of its architectural pleasures alone over its comparatively short history has not been made since the publication of Victorian engravings. It has received only one recent somewhat disparaging account.[2]

What has happened since the Great War has, alas! happened all over the country and endless acres of council and speculative building on the periphery are similar to those elsewhere and bear little or no relation to the indigenous architecture of Tunbridge Wells in particular. Factory-made building components are distributed in every direction, and the bright new estates of Tunbridge Wells are those of many other towns.

Even the railway that cut its way through the heart of the town did less physical damage than have subsequent intrusions. A substantial book could be written about the alien buildings of Tunbridge Wells and other resorts, fewer on their Continental counterparts. The railway brought

xiv

commercial prosperity, but a commercially prosperous town is often an ugly one. Uncouth buildings have recently blundered into picturesque groups and terraces; modest but charming pairs of stuccoed Regency villas have been mutilated and decay before our eyes; vast 'architecturalised' office blocks of liver-coloured brick and strips of glass and stained concrete still rise. In the 1930s Burton's celebrated stone houses in Calverley Park were separated from his stone church by a mountain of contemporary brick, thus marring the landscaped unity of this unique piece of town planning. The great green valley south-west of the town is now choked by ribbon-type development and from its far side the dramatic prospect of Mount Ephraim on the facing height is utterly diminished and can only be glimpsed over a sea of standard red roofs or through an occasional narrow gap.

Unlike the resorts of Bath and Brighton, Tunbridge Wells has no overall plan, but valuable patches of distinction. That these patches still remain is in no small measure due to the diligence of the Civic Society, sometimes with the help of the Borough and County Councils, fighting a continual battle against ignorance and ill-conceived commercial and other planning projects.

Basically the town is an amalgam; some of its cottages, terraces and more imporant buildings could be interchanged happily with those in Lewes, Rye, or St. Leonards. It grew up before the advent of classical planning, and by the time Burton was transforming the wooded slopes of Mount Pleasant into a *rus in urbe* paradise, The Picturesque Theory, based on romantic, pictorial irregularity, had superseded formality. In the 17th century the Wells and the ravishing scenery alone drew visitors from afar, buildings following solely to accommodate those taking the waters, attending the festivities arranged round them and exploring the mysterious rock formations in the strange countryside beyond. Numerous elegant lodging-houses were built for the Seasons organised by Beau Nash and these illustrate the architectural nature of the old town before the arrival of Burton. When the popularity of the waters waned, its fame as a beauty-spot reasonably near to London was firmly established. The old lodging-houses became permanent homes; even larger mansions appeared on Mount Ephraim and in the surrounding landscape; estates of modest family houses were built on idyllic sites; palaces in Italianate style dominated the skyline and Nature and Man combined to make Tunbridge Wells the ideal picturesque country town. William Plomer described the Common and High Rocks as 'two of the most adventurous places in England'.

Modern Tunbridge Wells is rich in recreational and social activities. It has its own facilities for opera, a symphony orchestra, choral society and innumerable clubs for sport and entertainment. Some of these might have been housed in existing buildings of interest, such as the Great Hall of 1870—the visitor's first sight of the town's High Victorian exuberance when arriving by train—or Burton's 'redundant' church, still struggling to command the town, as intended, although now jostled by new neighbours of dismal uniformity. But decay and rebuilding continue to the detriment of the town's indigenous qualities.

This said, the inquiring and imaginative visitor can even so enjoy an extraordinary country townscape. He must avert his eyes from the undistinguished, the unsuitable and the bad and seek what remains of its earlier nature. This is the Tunbridge Wells of weatherboarding, weathertiling and stucco. Its immensely varied architectural progress ranges from the smallest old cottage to the plaster mansion set among spreading cedars.

T.D.

# Outline History

TUNBRIDGE WELLS is not an old town. It has no ancient church or castle; only by 1740 had it, so to speak, grown up in the form of a spa fashionable enough to rival Bath. The town is unique and resembles no other in the country. 'Tunbridge Wells', wrote Samuel Crisp to Fanny Burney in 1779, 'is a place that appeared to me very singular. The country is all rock, and every part of it is either up or down hill; . . . the houses too are scattered about in a strange, wild manner, as if they had been dropped by accident, for they form neither streets nor squares'.[1] This is the essence of the town—romantic irregularity, untamed surroundings, an accidental, precocious tribute to The Picturesque Theory itself.

Because the various centres of the town are so scattered, it is difficult to appreciate its extraordinary situation and the casual visitor is apt to imagine that either of the three 'villages' of which the town is composed is *the* village, *the* centre. The Wells were discovered before the formal streets and squares of London were laid out, and it took many years for this type of planning to spread to country towns. The Pantiles containing the Wells[2] were the nearest thing to a market square that the town was ever to possess —long tree-shaded walks with little attempt at formality. All accounts of Tunbridge Wells must start with Eridge, a seat of the Barons of Bergavenny,[3] some two miles away and hidden in dense woodland and forest. Indeed, it is because Eridge existed at all that the spa was founded. In the early 17th century the primitive old house was used mainly as a hunting-lodge and it was to this remote place that Lord North at the age of 25 retreated from the dissipations of the Court of James I.[4] Before that Queen Elizabeth had stayed at the house for a week at the time she was becoming infatuated with her 'little frog'—the dwarf son of Catherine de Medici, over 20 years her junior. We may assume, therefore, that the house, although rough and simple was the scene of considerable hospitality and that visitors occupied themselves hunting in Waterdown Forest, then part of the vast Bergavenny estates and now occupied by the southern regions of Tunbridge Wells. The valley that to this day divides the town had, at its northern end, the hamlet of Southborough and at its southern, the forests and wild surroundings of Eridge.

Lord North derived no benefit from his self-imposed exile in the country and, we are told, took leave of his host at Eridge and rode sadly back to London in 1606 through these forests. Nearing the entrance to the valley, he came across a Chalybeate (iron-impregnated) pool of water, its strange colour and quality reminding him of that at Spa in France which he had earlier visited. Its colour was due to the many iron foundries in the district and he took a sample back to London for analysis in the belief that the waters might have properties to cure not only his own maladies, but also those of others suffering from all manner of disorders. North's physician declared the water to contain 'vitriol'—considered of great medicinal value. It 'cured', according to the accepted opinion of the day, 'the colic, the melancholy, and the vapours; it made the lean fat, the fat lean; it killed flat worms in the belly, loosened the clammy humours of the body, and dried the over-moist brain'.[5]

He soon returned to Eridge for a course of the waters and, feeling some-what better after the treatment, many of his friends at Court followed him and began to flock to the spring. Thus began the history of Tunbridge Wells.

A small cottage situated near the spring was all that marked the spot later to be known as the Walks, the Parade, the Royal Parade, Ye Olde Pantyles and finally the Pantiles. Thirty years were to pass, however, after Lord North's discovery in 1606 before adequate accommodation was built or made available for those taking the waters, and in the meantime they lodged in scattered cottages, huts and encampments on Bishop's Down on the northern slope of the valley, now the Common, that divides Sussex from Kent. Other accommodation was found in the nearby hamlets of Rusthall and Southborough. The valley continued in the direction of the ancient town of Tunbridge[6] about six miles away, where rooms of less primitive nature could be rented.

When the fame of the waters spread they naturally became a new centre of activity and by the mid 1630s a walk and a few wooden buildings

2

appeared—the first sign of architecture to appear. This precinct was to remain, through many changes, the basic plan of a parade focused on the waters where later the fashionable world would stroll under the avenue of tall trees, drink coffee, sample wares from market stalls, gossip, gamble and sometimes forget that the purpose of their visit was to take quantities of the iron-flavoured waters.

The impressive cavalcade of distinguished visitors began in 1630 when Queen Henrietta Maria stayed for six weeks to recover from the birth of her second son, later Charles II, and the Court camped in tents on Bishop's Down. The festivities devised for her visit were elaborate and rumbustious, contrasting with the comparatively refined entertainments required by lesser mortals a century later.

In 1636 two buildings were erected near the Wells—a coffee-house for ladies and a 'pipe-office' for the gentlemen. A Dr. Lodwick Rowzee[7] of Ashford took it upon himself to advise visitors on taking the waters, preferably in large quantities, and strongly recommended smoking afterwards.

But the Civil War put an end to all such thoughts and for a time the neighbourhood was over-shadowed by the conflict. The hamlet of Rusthall became the haunt of the Roundheads, Southborough that of the Royalists.

With the Restoration begins a serious attempt to transform a row or two of makeshift buildings adjacent to the Wells into a scene attractive enough to please sophisticated visitors, chiefly from London, who were preparing for a time of post-Civil War prosperity. It was not long after the Restoration that Charles II and Catherine of Braganza came to the Wells for two months in 1663, staying in a house on Mount Ephraim, their retinue in tents on the Common. Lord Muskerry, owner of the great Elizabethan house, Somerhill, near Tunbridge, was their constant host. The Somerhill estate extended to the limits of the Wells from the north and, although there were complicated litigations as to ownership, Muskerry took it upon himself to restore and improve the appearance of the Wells, erecting an entrance arch emblazoned with his arms. The lavish entertainment that Muskerry heaped upon Charles II and Catherine of Braganza only enhanced the reputation of the Wells. Nothing could now stem the tide of distinguished patronage.[8]

The Royal visits encouraged the laying out of bowling greens, bowling having become the most popular pastime, at Rusthall, Southborough and Mount Ephraim. Assembly rooms and coffee and lodging houses also sprang up in these outlying districts. In 1670 the Duke of York (later James II) and his family made High Rocks their favourite highly picturesque place to visit and soon their popularity necessitated a rest house being built there.

By 1678 the first Church of England was completed, known as 'the Chapel of Ease'. It was dedicated to King Charles the Martyr and enlarged in 1688–96. Churches and chapels gradually replaced the meeting-houses of other sects of dissenters.

Towards the end of the century the Pantiles were being greatly improved. A broad grass bank 175 yards long was raised, stretching south-west from the Wells forming the Upper Walk. An avenue of tall trees was planted in the centre for shade and dividing it from the lower walk devoted mostly to a provisions market and a band-stand.

The Upper Walk consisted of more substantial wooden buildings with over 20 good shops under a continuous colonnade with assembly rooms and lodgings above. Under the trees local tradesmen sold souvenirs and local wares.

In 1698 Princess Anne made her second visit and owing to her son the Duke of Gloucester's fall on the muddy Walks, gave £100 for paving them with Pantiles.[9] On returning a year later the Princess was so dismayed to find no tiles laid on the Walks that she never visited the town again. The Upper Walk was paved in 1700 and by 1706 there were two taverns near the Wells. There was no attempt at architectural uniformity, although several of the buildings had their own distinct charm and the whole scene was beginning to take the shape and style that was to become so widely famed. The origins of nearly Mount Zion as a popular site are dramatic; wooden houses of basic structure were moved wholesale on sleighs down the valley from Mount Ephraim to be re-erected in this new-found setting. Tradesmen followed in their wake and old Tunbridge Wells, as we know it today, was formed. The town would spread in every direction, Mount Ephraim would reign supreme because of its dominant position, but Mount Sion and the village that grew up with it became Tunbridge Wells.

Social as well as the first signs of architectural elegance were established when Beau Nash, after his triumphs at Bath, made Tunbridge Wells his new

4

centre as Master of Ceremonies. But first he had to wait for the death in 1735 of the formidable Bell Causey, long established as the fund-raiser for the various entertainments and conductor of the gaming-room. She was both popular and successful and there was no question of Nash usurping her territory. It was in 1736, therefore, that Nash organised the most sumptuous Season, attracting 1,000 resident visitors in six weeks. According to the diaries of Thomas Wilson, a London clergyman, 'seven dukes, duchesses and their daughters; thirty-three marquesses, earls, barons, their wives, children and relatives; sixteen knights, their ladies, children, etc. 3 M.P.s: 3 colonels and ten other persons of social distinction'[10] could be counted in the first week. In fact, more distinguished people visited Tunbridge Wells in its zenith than any other town in the country. Nash saw to it that the medicinal properties of the waters took second place to the entertainment of high society, and the visitors quickly began to appreciate the rustic surroundings, although, of course, sophisticated requirements equal to those found in Bath, were provided inside the simple buildings erected for accommodation and amusement. The three Mounts remained separate villages and exploring the delights of each was all part of the Season's activities.

Nash's loyal followers from Bath soon helped other visitors to fit into the impresario's strict code of manners, and the gaming-rooms (the most important haunts), ballrooms and coffee houses were organised with a new brilliance. But the visitors, according to rank and wealth, were harried by an endless list of subscriptions; nothing was free. They paid to enter all public rooms, in which to talk and read, to hear music elsewhere, to attend the two weekly balls, to sit in a coffee house, to have the Pantiles swept. Since many attempted to avoid these payments Nash imported a formidable woman touter—Sarah Porter—who, cash-book in hand, would follow defaulters round the public rooms until they paid up. The assembly rooms were continually being enlarged to accommodate the ever-increasing numbers of visitors. In 1745 French, Portuguese, Hungarians, and Italians joined the scene.

Nash's reign lasted from 1736-1755, and during this time all three Mounts had developed although most of the early-mid-18th century houses have vanished and only a few examples and fragments, mostly concealed behind later facades, are of his period. He devoted his last summers to the town and died at Bath in 1761 aged eighty-seven. He had been able to combine those two disparate qualities—amusement and politeness—more successfully than anyone in 18th-century society.

After Nash's death, Tunbridge Wells had passed its peak of popularity as a brilliant spa but remained a centre for relaxation and diversion and became what might be called 'a late-18th-century resort', where Society still assembled for amusements.

But times and Tunbridge Wells were changing. The second half of the 18th century still had its glittering moments, such as a few days' visit by the brothers of George III in 1765, who were greeted with gun salutes and elaborate illuminations in the Pantiles. In 1770, a Mrs. Baker opened the first theatre, cricket was played on the Common, and in 1778 John Wesley preached to the serious members of the inhabitants and visitors and he noted that 'deep attention sat on every face'.[11] In other words, the town was becoming a permanent community. People were deciding to live in rather than merely visit the place. In the 1789s the coach-ride to London was about seven hours. Fewer shops remained seasonal (May to October) and the chapel was opened throughout the year. Houses of distinction had been built, the most important being Mount Pleasant House of 1762 for the Earl of Egmont and later purchased by the Duke of Leeds;[12] others emerged on Mount Sion, many now demolished, and on Mount Ephraim, some of which are buried within the solid walls of the present large hotels.

Some of these substantial houses were, of course, let to the aristocracy and others of means for periods equivalent to the old Seasons, but scenes of natural beauty and wonder like High Rocks a mile away and the good air became as important as the amusements in the Pantiles. It was simply a pleasant place in which to spend a holiday, soon to be deserted in favour of Brighton when sea bathing became the fashion.

At the beginning of the 19th century, various enlargements and improvements were made to two of the main original hotels—the Sussex Tavern and the Kentish. Donkey-riding, introduced by Lady George Seymour, became very popular, Mrs. Baker's theatre flourished, and Edmund Kean, then aged 19, appeared in her company. The Bath House, a pleasing classical building, was built in 1804, but its success was short-lived and by 1840 had become a lodging-house and shop.

Roads had long been improved between Tunbridge and the Wells, and it was no longer necessary for the great houses of Penshurst, Eridge and Somerhill to apologise for local, crude access. Tunbridge Wells had now changed from a seasonal spa into a residential town for the upper classes and city merchants of discernment. These new residents were less frivolous and amusement-bent than the visitors of the previous century. Many were hard-headed businessmen rising on the tide of the Industrial Revolution— sober dignitaries of a future Royal town.

Princess Victoria (who was later to visit the town as Queen) came for a second visit with her mother, the Duchess of Kent, in 1834 and again stayed at Mount Pleasant House. Decimus Burton's important Calverley Estate on the Mount was well under way in the early 1830s and architectural and domestic respectability was rapidly becoming established. Solid dignity was replacing temporary elegance.

Burton's dominating Holy Trinity, completed in 1829, was the first church to supplement the now inadequate Chapel of Ease. Many others followed to supply the demand of new residential areas that were developed after the extension of the South-Eastern to the town in the mid-1840s.[13] Even before this, from 1810-41, the population had increased from about fifteen hundred to eight thousand.

The Victorians built in extravagant style. William Willicombe, successor to Decimus Burton, laid out new residential roads of small family houses from the 1860s, estates of much larger ones and palatial mansions in magnificent grounds. The late 19th century provided one of the most beautiful entrances to any town in the country—Pembury Road—where the great houses were concealed by the splendid trees that still remain. Once the town spilled subtly into the country and the country was beckoned gently into the town.

After the completion of the railway the town was open to a flood of new residents. When Edward VII granted the prefix 'Royal' to the Borough in 1909, the population was 35,000; today it is about fifty thousand.

1. Weatherboarded shops and houses in the 'village' of Mount Ephraim.

# I

# Mount Ephraim

MOUNT EPHRAIM, so named, like Mount Sion, during the Puritan Commonwealth period, is the most commanding position in the area and was chosen partly for this reason, no doubt, for the first visits of royalty to the Wells. The Mount is both strategic and spectacular. The Courts pitched their tents at the extreme western end of the hill (virtually a long ridge) known as Bishop's Down, but, for the purposes of visual pleasure we will start at the other extreme end, with the morning sun behind, where the first glimpse of the Regency town is seen on arrival from London. Nothing now remains of the buildings erected in the 17th and early 18th centuries.

The first existing buildings comprise in fact, the 'village' of Mount Ephraim, where pubs, shops, restaurants and other facilities are found in

8

2. A Victorian shopfront added to an earlier building.

4. Mount Ephraim from the Common. The castellated villas and the pedimented Royal Wells Inn are among the buildings that survive.

one short street of architectural interest. The weather-boarded buildings (1) are a refreshing contrast to most of what we see in St. John's Road which joins them from the north.

Perhaps the Victorian chemist's shop (2) catches the eye most easily, but opposite, dumped in the middle of earlier houses, is a miniature 'Jacobean' red-brick confection of *c.* 1870. Through a gap between the George Inn and other good houses is one of the best views of Holy Trinity tower.

On leaving the 'village' one has two main options—to carry on along the ridge of Mount Ephraim or swoop down into the green expanse of the Common.[1] We take the former road and see the whole of the main part of present Tunbridge Wells spread out on the other side of the valley beyond the Common. Strange rock formations with picturesque cottages, 'Gibraltar' and 'St. Helena', built into them appear on the left and on the right a good

11

3. A contrast of stucco
and weathertiling.

jumble of weather-tiled houses and a semi-detached pair of castellated Regency villas (3) surveying the view. Some of these buildings can still be identified in the engraving of 1854 (4), but from now on much of what exists is of later date, not all of it worthy of note. A few Regency buildings survive amongst a number of large Edwardian tile-hung, balcony-bedecked lumps, some with a hint of George Devey[2] who worked in the town. The weather-tiled houses and castellated villas are the beginning of a series of buildings of many styles and dates facing south-west and make up the striking silhouette seen from Forest Road on the facing ridge. To enjoy them it is best to walk on the edge of the Common.

After a pair of large semi-detached red brick houses of the late 19th century with 'Tudor' overtones and weather-tiling, is the courtyard of the Royal Wells Inn,[3] a building of 1834 and of much character, with an enormous coat-of arms on the parapet. Unfortunately, the exterior is now overlaid with later bays and the interior completely altered. Next are two stuccoed houses of the same date, one with a Tuscan porch. Further on is a terrace of three large stuccoed Regency houses which, from a distance, resemble one great mansion with three generous bows. The two western houses have twin plain Tuscan porches and broad fanlights, the eastern house (probably added later) with narrower door and fluted pilasters makes the elevation asymmetrical. Adjacent is a short, bright terrace of four later houses with scalloped, decorative tile-hanging and next to it a handsome composition, probably by William Willicombe, of three large houses with balustraded bays. This is followed by a semi-detached pair, smaller in scale and of the same date.

After the junction of Molyneux Park Road, leading to the network of 'Merrie England' developments behind the ridge from the mid-19th century to the present day, we are faced with the surprising hulk of what is now known as Reliance House,[4] a large mansion of 1866 origin, greatly enlarged towards the skies at a later date in brilliant, balustraded red brick with pilastered decorations. It is the most prominent and flamboyant building on the Mount and makes a strange neighbour to a tiny, charming Regency lodge standing behind the massive stone wall of a vanished 18th-century house, its site tantalizingly marked by great cedars and beech.

12

5. 'Bredbury' of 1867 enjoys distant views over rocks, common and town.

6. A small stuccoed neo-Greek villa of the Regency.

The important yellow brick mansion, 'Bredbury', with its commanding tower (5) gives an idea of the scale on which the Victorians built outside the groups of houses in private estates. From Camden Hill on the other side of the valley it appears to be standing isolated in its own park—the Common, rocks and trees in the foreground.

In complete contrast, next come a small, square modern box belonging to another environment and one of the prettiest small villas in the town, neo-Greek, neat and self-possessed (6). Ugliness follows in a pair of semi-detached red brick houses of the 1890s, relief in a nice detached stuccoed late-Regency house and a larger, later one.

Here we are opposite Mount Edgecombe, one of the few groups of buildings on the Common, including a weather-boarded hotel and Mount Edgecombe Cottage, Gothick, with steep, castellated gable in weather-boarding. On the Common, too, is Romanoff Lodge, a brick Victorian 'Tudor' house, with elaborate barge-boarding.

14

Back on the Mount we have now reached the long irregular stuccoed respectability of the Wellington Hotel, opened in 1875 and next to it a nice curiosity—a tall house with narrow front facing the Common and richly decorated side elevation at right-angles to the hotel. Its height is relative, for next to it is the low canopied facade of the wisteria-clad Chalet (7).

Mount Ephraim ends with the red brick mock-Jacobean Mount Ephraim House (its child we noted in the 'village'), the site of the first substantial house to be built in the town. Perhaps the stone wall may be the only visible, original sign of the place where Charles II stayed. It adjoins Bishop's Down, where his mother and her Court had camped 33 years earlier.

Bishop's Down Grove of *c.* 1765, purchased by Richard Yorke (a rich retired merchant known as 'Major York') has, like all other houses of the 18th century in the Mount Ephraim area, long been absorbed by later

7. The most western of the villas on the Mount.

8. Nevill Park, a private Victorian estate with a rural aspect still preserved.

building. Yorke's house forms the nucleus of the present Spa Hotel, opened in 1880. Bishop's Down leads to Langton Road, where many large mansions were built in the 19th century, and Rusthall with its curious rock formations.

Opposite the hotel, Major York's Road runs straight down to the Pantiles through a densely wooded part of the Common. It would be difficult to find a more beautiful road in the centre of any town. Because of its steeply undulating nature, the landscape here gave excellent opportunities for laying out private parks with country views outside the restrictions of the protected Common. At the top end of the road Nevill Park runs to the west and was developed by the Abergavenny family from the 1840s. Unlike Burton's earlier Calverley Park, these larger rival mansions form a convex crescent and face Hungershall Park (also developed by the Abergavennys) across a wooded valley and lush green meadows, still farmed and used for grazing (8, 9).

The planning of Nevill park, considered by Professor A. E. Richardson to be Burton-controlled,[5] contains houses mostly in the Italianate style

16

9. The houses in Nevill Park are set
in spacious gardens.

10. Hungershall Park, facing Nevill Park across the fields.

which spread so rapidly all over the town from the end of the 1830s on so many different scales. Gothic Revival did not appear in earnest for secular building until the planning of nearby Broadwater Down from the 1860s and the five houses in the upper part of Calverley Park Gardens.

In Hungershall Park (10, 11) the houses are of a more wayward and sometimes eccentric, perhaps sinister, appearance, in styles difficult to define and nearly all determined to be highly individual. Both parks were still being developed well into the 1880s and now holly, laurel and yew increase their sense of exclusivity and seclusion. The grand Hungershall Park houses bend towards the south and end at the less grandly-named Cabbage Stalk Lane. A few yards west and we are immediately in open farmland on the way to High Rocks (12), one of the most dramatic surprises so near to any inland English town.

18

11. No. 2 Hungershall Park has rich
mouldings filled with coloured cera-
mic tiles.

12. High Rocks which have attracted visitors since the Wells were first discovered.

# II
# Mount Sion

THE LITERAL, PHYSICAL MIGRATION of fashion and its attendant trade from Mount Ephraim to Mount Sion after the Restoration saw the founding of a completely new village within walking distance of the Wells. Nothing now remains of the timber-framed, ramshackle buildings that were

13. The weatherboard clock tower and cupola of the Church of King Charles the Martyr, formerly the Chapel of Ease.

14. These buildings remain on Mount Sion although the canopies and other details
have disappeared from the tall bow-fronted villas.

wheeled down the valley, but we may suppose that they remained for several
years on the sides of the lane leading up the hill, where one or two larger
houses had been built, until they were gradually replaced by the Georgian
and Regency houses we see today. Most of these new buildings were used
entirely as lodging-houses until the end of the 19th century. Of these, several

22

15. Yellow brick bow fronts
on the north side of the hill.

17. Jerningham House, one of the earlier lodging-houses on the hill, has been altered over the years and the weathertiling is composed of decorative shapes, popular in the late 19th century.

have been demolished and some disfigured, but on the north side a group of interesting houses of considerable variety which Christopher Hussey has called 'the best Georgian sequence in the town', creeps up the hill.[1] Indeed they form a remarkable and diverse parade, including a small weatherboard cottage, a pair of tall bow-fronted stuccoed villas (14), a substantial yellow brick house with undulating bows (15), and two classical mansions, one with a curiously grotesque porch. Some have lost their ironwork and other important details, but the group is mostly intact. Behind it are smaller houses and cottages in narrow streets and alleys leading down to the High Street, forming a village in themselves. Many of the older cottages survive, others replaced from the mid-late 19th century by terraces of stuccoed houses.

On the lower south side of Mount Sion is Howard Lodge, a good brick house with broad fluted pilasters (16) and next to it Jerningham House of earlier date, with red weather-tiling and a generous supply of sash

16. Howard Lodge, an early 19th-century house with fluted giant pilasters.

windows, recently restored (17). At the top of the hill stand two impressive detached houses, Forest Prospect and Marlborough House, once commanding splendid views of Waterdown Forest to the south but now overlooking the rooftops of Edwardian and later buildings. Forest Prospect (now called Ivy Chimneys), an early 18th-century tile-hung timber-framed house, contains a fine panelled dining-room and a drawing-room formed out of the semi-circular bow of later date (18). Marlborough House (c. 1810) has a severe stuccoed north front with giant Corinthian pilasters, but the garden front pushes its bow windows and exotic verandah towards the lawns and cedars behind[2] (19).

At this point the road bends sharply to the left with neat terraces of small Victorian villas leading to the Grove. This piece of common ground was given to the public in 1705 by the self-styled 'Earl of Buckingham', son of Lady Muskerry of Somerhill, the large neighbouring estate. It became a favourite secluded retreat for those staying nearby during the Seasons and Betsy Sheridan, sister of the dramatist, described it in 1785 as consisting of 'venerable Oaks, Beach and Elm, all of such a size as to form a compleat shade at noon . . . this sweet spot is, I am told, quite deserted; no one walks but on the Pantiles'.[3]

Today the Grove resembles a miniature Clapham Common with small late-Victorian houses surrounding it. Some majestic trees have gone but it still provides a welcome green space in a now more built-up area. An adjacent terrace of older cottages emphasises the village atmosphere of this part of the hill (20).

Descending Mount Sion we pass the sites of Bedford House and Walmer House and turn left into Chapel Place, a pedestrian way of small shops mostly of Regency date, with the north side formed out of the 1878 rebuilding of the 18th-century Royal Kentish hotel. To the left again, parallel to Mount Sion, is Bedford Row (21), a terrace of tall houses also free of traffic and further down is glimpsed the neat, pious face of the Strict Baptist Chapel of 1851. But at the side of the church of King Charles the Martyr[4] with its elaborate Restoration ceilings and weather-boarded tower and cupola (13, 28) another path leads to Cumberland Walk[5] which contains houses of immediate appeal. Nos 6 (22) and 7, both early 19th century, are almost identical in design with 'Tudor' labels over Gothick-

27

18. Originally called Forest Prospect, parts
of this house are early 18th century.

glazed sashes and their stuccoed facades incised in imitation of stone. But No. 7 is provided with giant pilasters and the strange ammonite capitals used by the architect Amon Henry Wilds in Brighton and Lewes. Next door is a splendid four-storey house of about the same period but faced with cobbles and its windows and door surrounded by rubbed brick, a strange contrast to its neighbours (*frontispiece*). Further along the Walk are more modest houses and cottages of varying dates and some faced with weather-boarding; a terrace of late-Victorian houses completes the stretch of old buildings in this elevated position. Once it overlooked its own small valley, now filled with later housing, containing the stream that divided Kent from Sussex, towards Waterdown Forest, part of which is now occupied by that splendid avenue of rapidly-vanishing Victorian mansions—Broadwater Down. Its church of St. Mark, of 1846-6 (23), by R. L. Roumieu, sets the seal on this once most fashionable of roads.

Chapel Place links the Pantiles with the High Street, originally called the 'Foot of Mount Sion', then a country lane winding up to the densely-wooded hill to be known as Mount Pleasant. In 1808 there were only three houses on the east side and a few on the west. The street was created to supplement the market facilities of the Pantiles, still the busiest quarter, and its modest beginnings can be seen in the small weather-boarded shops at its lower end (24), remarkable and valuable survivals of this basically late-Georgian village. The patrons of the Wells were thus provided with another parade and a new architectural scene.

The street follows the upward curve of the Common until it reaches the railway station and was developed piecemeal as the area prospered and the town became more permanently residential at the end of the 18th century. The lanes to the south-east lead, as we have seen, to the 'village' lanes of Mount Sion, and the short streets on the opposite side to the London Road and the unspoiled vastness of the Common.

In spite of some miraculous earlier survivals, the High Street is mainly mid-19th century in feeling and character. By this time it was a thriving shopping centre. York House remains, a good, simple stuccoed Regency building (but partly obscured by a later addition), as do a number of bow-fronted buildings of modest proportions on the west side. But modern shop fronts and wayward fascia-boards attempt to overpower the upper

29

19. Marlborough House, a large lodging-house at the top of the hill built for visitors to the Regency Seasons.

21.  Bow windows in Bedford Row leading off Chapel Place.

parts of earlier, less brash inspirations, in particular the attractive neo-Classical terrace of shops, probably by Willicombe, adjacent to the dramatic, unexpected yellow brick Christ Church by Robert Palmer Brown of 1835-41 with its great neo-Norman stone arched portico (25). But, overlooking certain unfortunate intrusions of this century, the High

20. Houses off the Grove that form
part of the 'village' of Mount Sion.

23. St. Mark's Church, Broadwater Down.

Street became and remains to this day the pleasing shopping centre of the older part of the town and contains buildings of architectural value.

At its lower end the High Street bends towards the Common and on turning left past the former Royal Kentish Hotel, we see the opening to the Pantiles across Nevill Street. The latter is now unfortunately a busy main road leading to routes for Eastbourne and Hastings. Earlier it had been a quiet country lane to Frant and Eridge, scarcely disturbing the original town's most valuable group of buildings: the church, the Bath House and the Pantiles—in fact, its heart.

33

22. No. 6 Cumberland Walk, a
classical house with Gothick details.

24. Early survivals of weatherboarded buildings on the lower slope of the High Street.

Although the Pantiles are chronologically the origin of Tunbridge Wells, geographically they form part of the later residential development of Mount Sion, when the Wells were at the height of their popularity. From the humble beginnings of wooden structures to the later more sophisticated buildings, the immediate appeal of the Pantiles is their informality—the result of many years of haphazard building and re-building. The only linking element is the continuous colonnade of the north side and even this is made up of columns dating from the 17th century to the present day (26). This regiment in turn supports buildings of the utmost contrast in date, style and scale, presenting a scene of radiance, richness and entertainment. It is a feast and a pageant, to be enjoyed under the shade of tall limes in summer, under the shelter of the colonnade in winter.

On closer inspection the earlier survivals become apparent: the remaining late 17th-century wooden column of No. 48 (26), the little wine shop near the Bath House with its bow windows, and various tile-hung and certain weather-boarded upper parts on the north side. Nos. 14–16 were built in 1664. They have been changed through the years, but remain an attractive group. Most of the rest is later; even the worn flagstones of 1793 replace

34

25. The High Street in the mid-19th century with Christ Church on the left and William Willicombe's terrace of shops below, a scene still reasonably intact.

London J Harwood 26 Fenchurch St.

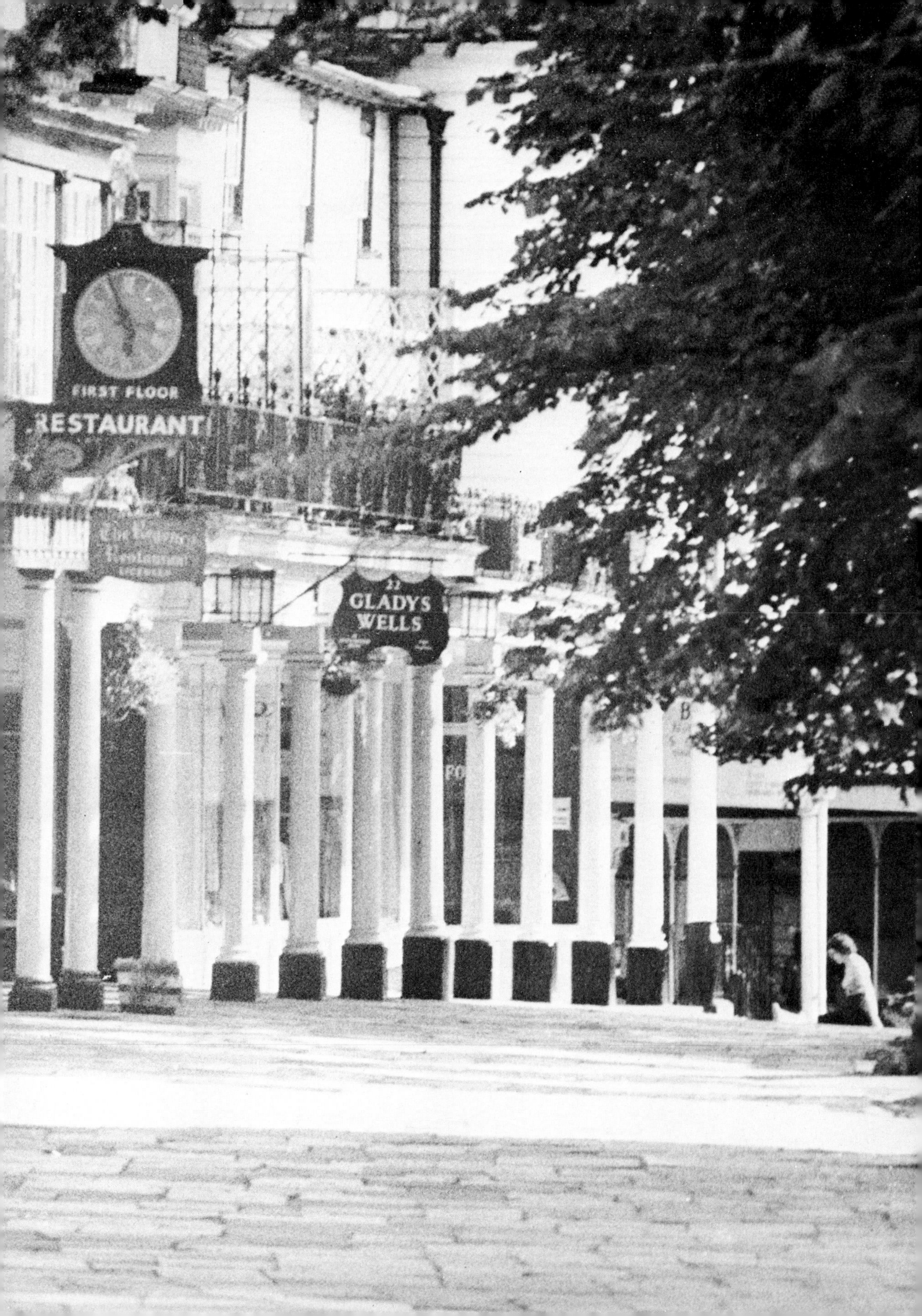
FIRST FLOOR
RESTAURANT
22
GLADYS
WELLS

Queen Anne's pantiles, only a group of which remains near the steps of Bath Square. Visitors will choose their favourite buildings from this eclectic parade, ignoring the few flies in the amber.

The southern end of the Pantiles is now entirely blocked off by Union House, a new, brooding complex of shops and offices. It replaces the late-Victorian Pump Room but, unfortunately, unlike the highly successful new square off the Lanes in Brighton where weather-boarding prevails, building materials quite alien to its neighbours are used here.

On the Lower Walk of the Pantiles its nearest neighbours are a good row of small stuccoed Regency houses; on the Upper Walk the mellowed weather-tiling of Binns, an old-established restaurant. Contrast can be successful, but these new buildings darken the essential lightness of the whole area.

The row of Regency houses, some with excellent iron balconies, joins the Royal Victoria and Sussex Hotel, now used as offices (27), where Princess Victoria stayed with her mother, whose massive coat-of-arms still weighs heavily but impressively over the door. At the back of the building remain the Assembly Rooms of early 19th-century social activities. The next building, the Corn Exchange, with its skyline statue of Ceres, goddess of corn, flanked by cornucopia, was once Mrs. Baker's Theatre of 1802. After that another terrace of stuccoed houses faces the end of the embankment and the old Coach and Horses, now an antique shop, but once the lodgings for visitors' servants. All the buildings we see today on the Lower Walk are in the area previously used by local tradesmen and country people as a produce market. The embankment between the Walks was built up in the 1890s.

Past the Coach and Horses the Lower Walk opens up into a small square upset only by its central feature, a mock-Tudor building on the site of the original fish-market, bearing the misleading legend 'Est. 1745'. It is a site crying out for a fountain, a statue of, say, Beau Nash, a tree or merely space from which to see the surrounding buildings: an elegant double bow-fronted house, the much-altered but still sympathetic Duke of York Tavern, and a formal Willicombe-type terrace of shops occupying the whole of the east side.

Back in Bath Square the Bath House itself, by J. T. Groves, of 1804, has been much altered and its most impressive facade opposite the Common

26. (Preceding pages). The colonnade in the Pantiles looking in the direction of Bath Square. Only one of the columns with tall black bases on the left is original.

27. The old Royal Victoria and Sussex Hotel on the Lower Walk of the Pantiles.

28. Only the Church of King Charles the Martyr (centre) remains from this group of buildings at the lower end of the London Road.

with giant pilasters, spectacular fanlight spanning twin openings and urn-studded parapet has been mutilated beyond recognition.

We now leave the Pantiles and cross over to the Common in order to complete the tour of the Mount Sion area. In this way we may include a very long stretch of buildings which face the Common on the London Road and back on to the High Street and Mount Pleasant Road—the latter stretch strictly belonging to Mount Pleasant.

Opposite the edge of the Common is the site of the old Royal Kentish Hotel (28), long replaced by the South Kensington-French pile containing a grand entrance hall with rich plasterwork and yellow scagliola Corinthian columns. The south end of the High Street then joins the London Road, containing some pleasant early 19th-century houses and shops with lodgings above. As we have noted, short streets join the London Road to the High Street, longer ones to Mount Pleasant Road as the main road curves to the west and then bends north alongside the Common, ending at the east-west Mount Ephraim Road. In this area are many secret gardens.

Further on is the much-rebuilt tile-hung Castle Hotel, originally of 1821, then a long terrace of tall stuccoed houses and The Methodist church in a grim Gothic of 1873. We then see The Kent and Counties Club of 1909 in very bold 'Queen Anne' by Cecil Burns, an architect who provided much good traditional work for the town. From now on most of the larger houses and terraces serve as hotels, including the long terrace in red-brick Jacobean style and Richmond Terrace (29), a good example of a trim mid-Victorian terrace of houses with good ironwork and slender columns supporting the balcony. It is here that the scene opens out into an enormous village green and the remainder of the houses is well set back from the main road by a spacious expanse of grass giving them the impression of being part of the Common itself. Sheep grazed here until recent years.

29. Richmond Terrace, a trim Victorian composition, with the tower of Holy Trinity in the background.

30.  Jordan House, London Road, its upper
storeys supported on columns.

After Richmond Terrace the more interesting buildings include the stone, castellated Gothick house (originally known as Romanoff House School) of Burton style, two pairs of Regency houses, each pair with almost the equivalent of a pediment, but one pair altered too much for its original elevations to be appreciated. The 'Deep South' porch of No. 61 can be noted with great pleasure, a barrel-vaulted covered way and trellis linking the front door to an elaborately carved wood outer door. Two large semi-detached 'Willicombe' houses follow, then Jordan House (30) on the corner of Church Road, with its weather-tiled upper floors and formal elevation.

After Church Road, which contains a number of good buildings as well as two faceless new blocks, comes a sequence of late Georgian and Regency houses to rival those on Mount Sion. Set back in one of the largest front gardens is the much restored No. 69 London Road, handsome, of five bays and with weather-tiling to the first floor (31).

31. No. 69, London Road, half weathertiling, half stucco.

A pair of tall semi-detached bow-fronted houses should be noted, their stuccoed facades varying only in detail from the pairs on Mount Sion and a castellated pair on Mount Ephraim. No. 72 is perhaps the prettiest villa of all; its white weather-boarding is incised to imitate stone in order to give a more sophisticated impression and its Doric porch supports a lacy, canopied balcony. It also retains its correct glazing bars, so often missing in older sashes throughout the town (32).

Next comes a Victorian villa concealing behind its bay-windowed front the original weather-boarded house that would be seen in engravings before later development. After another pair of tall semi-detached Willicombe-type houses comes a huge red brick late-Victorian detached building, followed by a trim Regency house with good canopied balcony and Rock View Cottage, with white-painted weather-tiling and some attractive detail. Two large detached Edwardian houses lead to two vaguely Italianate detached houses.

Finally we reach Thackeray's yucca-guarded house (33), where the writer stayed for two months in the summer of 1860 and wrote: 'What a delicious

33.  Thackeray's House, *c.*1660 facing the northern
corner of the Common.

air breathes over the heath, blows the cloud shadows across it and murmurs
through the full-clad trees! Can the world show a land fairer, richer, more
cheerful? I see a portion of it when I look up from the window where I
write'.[6] The house is tile-hung from ground to roof, has generously wide
sash windows and a pedimented porch on slender columns. It faces the
rocks on the Common and the houses beyond on Mount Ephraim. It is the
last building we see in this varied panorama and the first to delight the eye
on passing through the Common from the direction of London.

32. Regency houses facing the Common,
overlooking their own 'village green'.

# III
# Mount Pleasant

34. Decimus Burton's dominant 'Perpendicular' Holy Trinity of 1829, built to serve the Calverley Park area.

35. The Congregational Church, Mount Pleasant of 1848, possibly by a local stonemason, Jabez Scholes.

AFTER CASTING a protective glance towards the French-style Great Hall by H. H. Cronk of 1870, opposite the railway station,[1] we should, to avoid disappointment, ascend Mount Pleasant Road, the continuation of the High Street, on the west side with eyes firmly averted to the right.

On the left are several shops of quality but words other than 'pleasant' come more readily to the mind when the buildings themselves are examined. A new block of grim, elephantine aspect makes matters worse.

On the east side, however, a stately stuccoed terrace of shops of the 1870s climbs the hill and although, as in most towns, the shop-fronts are now grotesquely at odds, the upper parts that remain, the Gothic Revival bank at the higher end, also by Cronk of 1880 and the trees are a welcome sight.

Having reached the crossroads at the top of the hill—Mount Pleasant itself —we might expect the impact of Decimus Burton's new town of the 1830s

36. What remains of once-elegant York Road is mostly on the north side (Nos 6-14, 40-42, 52-56).

to be the crowning glory of this wonderful site. Fifty years ago it was; today it is not. The 1930s passion for demolition and building 'on the splay' is well demonstrated in this commanding spot. For no easily determined reason the self-important Civic Centre by Percy Thomas and Ernest Prestwick of the late 1930s faces us on the north-east corner on an absurd scale and at an arrogant angle to its site replacing Burton's terraces of stone houses. Opposite, also at an inexplicable angle is the cinema, again of the 1930s and of totally undistinguished design. We have noted the bank, and opposite is a modern neo-classical building unhappily tacked on to the archway of the Gothick Priory of 1827. Adjacent is Burton's church (34), still grand, and containing what has been described as its impressive interior,[2] but now isolated from the Calverley Estate by the Civic Centre.

Over these unlovely crossroads and further along on the west side is the severe portico of the Congregational Church added in 1866 to an even more

48

37. Artisans' brick cottages in Camden Road, the northern
limit of the town in the 19th-century.

38. Mid-Victorian St. James's Church, a landmark in the eastern part of the Calverley Estate.

severe classical stone box (35). Opposite are the copper seaside domes of the Opera House of 1902 now, alas! used for entertainment requiring less skill than singing. The streets to the west leading to the top corner of the Common contain terrace houses of interest (36) and next to the Opera House is the curious Monson Colonnade of 1889 with its shops and continuous iron balcony.[3]

But where, a few yards on, Calverley, Grosvenor and Mount Ephraim roads join Mount Pleasant Road we have another area of chaos. It is somewhat worse than the crossroads just described, for it is almost beyond architectural analysis, and more congested. Calverley Road, now the busiest main shopping street in the town, contains the groups of Burton's sadly mutilated villas and shops designed to serve his Calverley

50

39. Doric and Roman elements at Victoria Gate, the main entrance to Calverley Park.

Estate. Here his Market House and other buildings of the 1830–40s have long been replaced. Camden Road, running north in the direction of the industrialised area of High Brooms, contains shops of early 19th-century origin and artisan cottages (37). To the west is a network of similar terraced cottages and to the east lie the spacious roads lined with Willicombe's handsome Victorian Italianate plaster villas and Ewan Christian's Gothic Revival St. James's Church of 1862 (38).

So we must return to the top of Mount Pleasant and turn east past the Civic Centre (which replaces Burton's Calverley Parade and Terrace), with the Calverley Hotel on the right. Ahead is Victoria Gate, the Doric and Roman stone archway to Burton's Calverley Park (39), and to the left the entrance to his Calverley Park Crescent. The story of the development of the Calverley Estate is remarkable.[4] Decimus Burton's father, who had a house near Tunbridge, was a colleague of John Nash and worked on many of his great London schemes. His son became a pupil of Nash and at a

40. The villas in Calverley Park with the hotel on the extreme left.

very early age was designing some of the Regent's Park buildings. His most familiar monument is the Ionic Hyde Park Corner screen but his London work was prodigious in many areas. Likewise in the Kent and Sussex countryside; and it is little wonder that John Ward, who had in 1825 acquired nearly 1,000 acres of farmland on Mount Pleasant (including a sandstone quarry) commissioned Decimus Burton to develop some 50 acres of the estate in 1827.

Burton, naving worked on Nash's Regent's Park scheme, where classical villas were set in romantic, picturesque surroundings, must have suggested a similar plan for Ward's land—the ideal, model separate estate where there would be houses overlooking parkland for the reception of 'genteel families'.[5] Nearby would be shops and all other facilities. In other words it was to rival the residential attractions of Mount Sion now that the Wells were no longer of first importance.

41. No. 2 Calverley Park with its verandah linking the two main blocks.

42. No. 1, Calverley Park.

43. No. 7, Calverley Park.

Between 1827-50 Burton designed 24 stone villas in Greek and Italianate styles placed in a grand sweep on the north-east summit of the hill (40) overlooking the 'old' town. The valley below was landscaped in the picturesque style with great cedars and groups of other trees and shrubbery providing an informal, 'natural' foreground. It was, and remains, the finest predecessor to all garden suburbs. In date it coincides almost exactly with the little Park Villages of Regent's Park. Most of the villas, set in their own gardens, are in Greek style (41, 44) some in a combination of Greek and Italiante, others deliberately made more picturesque and irregular by the inclusion of a tower element and emphatic bracketed eaves. The general style of the villas is classical, but the variations and mixtures of elements are subtle and as Christopher Hussey has noted, the Orders are absent except when they are functional. There is a discipline lacking in Regent's Park; basic shapes are crisp and controlled.

The Crescent (45) of 1835 adjacent to the west end of the Park is Mount Pleasant's answer to the Pantiles. Originally known as the Promenade, it was the meeting-place for local residents and their visitors. Its 17 houses face an elliptical lawn, gardens and trees. There was a fountain and a band played regularly in the summer. The colonnade, with its slender columns and gentle curve comprised shops on ground and basement floors, baths, a library and reading room. For a time it was the centre for genteel occupations; the middle classes had come to stay.

54

44. No. 11 Calverley Park. Slim iron columns support balconies in several of the villa compositions.

Rock & Co. London. No 1185

46. Lansdowne Road of the 1860s where medium-sized villas became very sought-after.

47. Large villas in Sandrock Road with St. James's Church in the distance.

45. (Preceding pages). Calverley Park Crescent, once the centre of social activities for the Park.

We owe most of the remainder of the Calverley Estate to Willicombe, apart from Burton the only person to develop 19th-century Tunbridge Wells in a comprehensive manner and on any scale. Indeed his output and influence were remarkable. His main contribution was the development of the eastern acres of the estate, where he laid out Lansdowne Road (46) with its compact medium-sized plaster villas with Italianate overtones, the larger ones in Sandrock Road (47), and some of the earlier very grand mansions in Calverley Park Gardens, some Gothic Revival (48), and others classical behind a splendid laurel-laden sloping stone wall worthy of Piranesi. He built palatial houses on the Calverley Fair Mile (now less attractively called Pembury Road) and supplied terraces of houses and shops in other parts of the town. Of humble origin from Bath, he was taken up by Burton and his builders whose basic classical tradition he carried on.

48. Four of the Gothic Revival houses in Calverley Park Gardens remain in a development predominantly classical in style.

49.  A stuccoed villa in Lansdowne Road where simplicity is combined with strong
architectural forms.

50. Detail of classical stucco
decoration in Lansdowne Road.

51. No. 1 Camden Park, a large house
overlooking parkland. The emphatic
bracketed eaves are common to most
of the Italianate designs.

52. No. 2 Camden Park, a house similar to those in neighbouring roads but in more spacious surroundings.

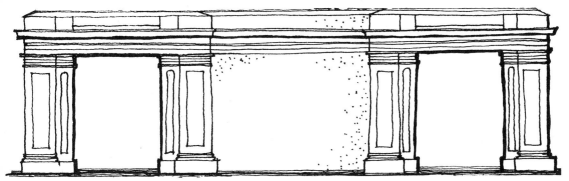

53. The simple stuccoed entrance arches to Grove Hill Gardens.

modified to suit the prevailing taste, in plaster rather than stone, but usually with detail of some richness (49, 50).

Again, because of the success of the Calverley Park houses, Willicombe also contributed to Camden Park to the east—another crescent of houses overlooking landscaped parkland, started but not completed by the Marquess Camden of nearby Bayham Abbey (51, 52).

Before leaving the Mount Pleasant area we should descend Camden Hill and note the very attractive group of stuccoed houses of the 1830s at the top of Grove Hill Road. The houses are laid out in a curve with entrances also in Claremont Road. The concave bow-fronted elevations face a small park and are approached by extremely simple archways (53, 54, 55). The group has suffered some mutilation, but even today its appeal remains. A few charming houses of the same period remain to be seen on the south side of Grove Hill Road, leading us back to the High Street; but most of the building is much later, with short streets of red-brick terrace houses leading to the Grove itself—that green haven so treasured by Georgian visitors to a spa of such original and magnetic personality.

54. End houses of Grove Hill Gardens.

55. The Claremont Road facades of
the houses in Grove Hill Gardens.

# NOTES

## Preface

1. The most recent are: Margaret Barton, *Tunbridge Wells* (1937), and Alan Savidge, *Royal Tunbridge Wells* (1975), a detailed and valuable account.
2. *The Buildings of England—West Kent and the Weald*, John Newman; ed. Nikolaus Pevsner (1969).

## Outline History

1. See H. R. Knipe (ed.), *Tunbridge Wells and Neighbourhood* (1916).
2. Only one well at the north end of the Pantiles was eventually used.
3. In the 18th century the name was changed to Abergavenny and in 1784 the 17th Baron was created an Earl.
4. The first account of North's visit was given by Thomas Benge Burr, a local resident, in 1766 and is the generally accepted account of the discovery of the Wells. North died in 1666 aged 85.
5. Margaret Barton, *op. cit.*
6. Now Tonbridge. The name was changed when the railway was built to avoid confusion between the two towns. It didn't; passengers to this day alight at Tonbridge thinking they have reached Tunbridge Wells. Originally the town might have been called Eridge Wells and it is said that Lord Abergavenny suggested Frant Wells after the nearest hamlet to Eridge. Eventually it took its name from the nearest town of importance.
7. After Queen Henrietta's visit he published *The Queen's Wells, that is, a Treatise of the Nature and Virtues of Tunbridge Water* (1632). It was re-published in 1671.
8. H. R. Knipe, *op. cit.*, although mostly devoted to flora, fauna and geology, includes a good account of events and visitors from 1606–1915.
9. A word derived from roofing tiles.
10. Alan Savidge, *op. cit.*
11. H. R. Knipe, *op. cit.*
12. Reconstructed by Decimus Burton as the Calverley Hotel in 1840.
13. There are now 35 churches of various denominations in the vicinity of the town.

## I.—Mount Ephraim

1. 250 acres of the Common were protected from building encroachment by an Act of Parliament in 1740.
2. A pupil of C. F. A. Voysey.
3. Originally the Hare and Hounds Inn.
4. Built for the Hon. F. G. Molyneux on the site of an older house. It became an hotel at the beginning of this century and is now used as offices.
5. *Early Victorian England*, Vol. 2, ed. G. M. Young (1934).

## II.—Mount Sion

1. *Country Life,* 12 December 1968.
2. Built on the site of the house of 1717 occupied by the Duke of Marlborough.
3. *Betsy Sheridan's Journal* (1781–1786 and 1788–1790), ed. William Le Fanu (1960).
4. See Alan Savidge, *The Church of King Charles the Martyr* (1969).
5. Probably named after Richard Cumberland, the dramatist, who lived on Mount Sion for 25 years.
6. From the *Cornhill Magazine* of which he was editor. See E. Yoxall Jones, *A Prospect of Tunbridge Wells* (1964).

## III.—Mount Pleasant

1. The 'up-side' building of the 1840s is now 'listed'.
2. *Collin's Guide to English Parish Churches,* ed. John Betjeman (1968).
3. The *art nouveau* Adult Education Centre by H. T. Hare of *c.*1900, also in Monson Road, should be noted.
4. For fuller recent accounts see Christopher Hussey: *Calverley Park, Tunbridge Wells,* 1, 8 May 1969; and Alan Savidge, *op. cit.*
5. J. Colbran, *Guide to Tunbridge Wells* (1840).

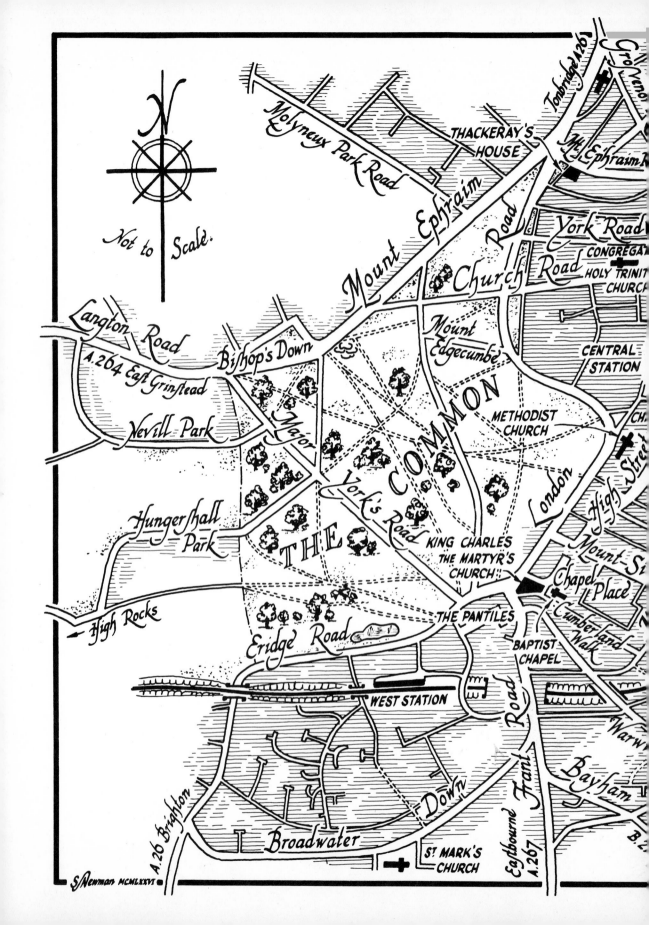

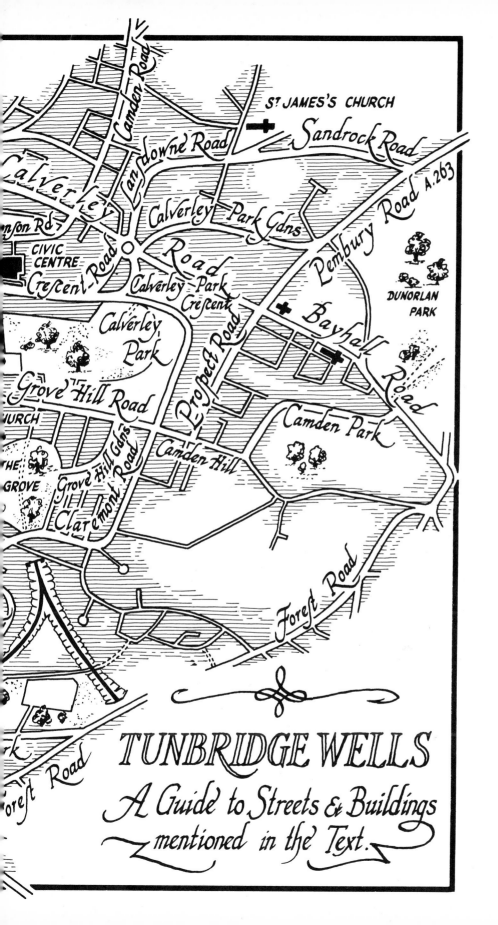

St JAMES'S CHURCH

Sandrock Road

Camden Road

Lansdowne Road

Pembury Road A.263

Calverley

Calverley Park Gdns

nson Rd.

CIVIC CENTRE

Road

Crescent Road

DUNORLAN PARK

Calverley Park Crescent

Bayhall Road

Calverley Park

Prospect Road

Grove Hill Road

Camden Park

HURCH

THE GROVE

Grove Hill Gdns

Claremont Road

Camden Hill

Forest Road

Forest Road

# TUNBRIDGE WELLS
## A Guide to Streets & Buildings mentioned in the Text.

69

# INDEX

George III, brothers of: 6
George Inn: 11
Gibraltar Cottage: 11
Great Hall, the: xiv, 47
Grosvenor Road: 50
Grove, the: 27, 63
Grove Hill Road: 63
Groves, J. T.: 38

Hastings: 33
Henrietta Maria, Queen: 3, 15
High Brooms: 51
High Rocks: xiv, 4, 6, 18
High Street: 25, 29, 31-3, 40, 47, 63
Holy Trinity Church: 7, 11
Howard Lodge: 25
Hungershall Park: 16, 18
Hussey, Christopher: 25, 54
Hyde Park Corner: 52

Iron foundries: 2

James I: 1
James II, as Duke of York: 4
Jerningham House: 25
Jordan House: 42

Kean, Edmund: 6
Kent and Counties Club: 41
Kent, Duchess of: 7
King Charles the Martyr, Church of: *see*
   Chapel of Ease

Langton Road: 16
Lansdowne Road: 59
Leeds, Duke of: 6
Lewes: xiii, 29
London: 6, 7, 45, 51
London Road: 29, 40, 42
Lower Walk: 38

Major York's Road: 16
Marlborough House: 27
Market House: 51
Molyneux Park Road: 12
Monson Colonnade: 50

Mount Edgecombe: 14
Mount Edgecombe Cottage: 14
Mount Ephraim: xi, xiii, 3-7, 11ff., 21,
   43, 45
Mount Ephraim House: 15
Mount Ephraim Road: 41, 50
Mount Pleasant: xi, xiii, 5, 7, 29, 40,
   51-2, 54
Mount Pleasant House: 6, 7
Mount Pleasant Road: 40, 47, 50
Mount Sion: xi, 4-7, 21ff., 34, 52
Muskerry, Lord: 3
Muskerry, Lady: 27

Nash, Beau: xiii, 4-6, 38
Nash, John: 51-2
Nevill Park: 16
Nevill Street: 33
North, Lord: 1

Opera House: 50

Pantiles, the: 1, 2, 4-6, 16, 29, 33-4, 38,
   40, 54
Pembury Road: 7, 59
Penshurst: 7
'Pipe office': 3
Piranesi: 59
Plomer, William: xiv
Porter, Sarah: 5
Prestwick, Ernest: 48
Priory, the: 48
Promenade, the: *see* Calverley Park
   Crescent
Pump Room: 38

Railway: *see* South-Eastern Railway
Regent's Park: 52-4
Reliance House: 12
Richardson, Professor A. E.: '16
Richmond Terrace: 41-2
Rock View Cottage: 43
Romanoff House School: 42
Romanoff Lodge: 14
Roumieu, R. L.: 29
Rowzee, Dr. Lodwick: 3